Taming Python

A Gentle Introduction
to Python Programming Language

Patty Belle

MP Publishing

Copyright

© 2017 by Patty Belle

Table of Content

I. Python Overview

Before getting started, let's get familiarized with the language first.

Python is a high-level, general purpose, interpreted, interactive, and object-oriented scripting language. It is engineered to make the programs you write easier to read. While other languages use punctuation, it frequently uses English keywords and it has lesser syntactical structures than other languages. It is fun to work in Python as it allows you to concentrate on the problem instead of focusing on the syntax.

Python is:

- **Interpreted:** Python is processed at runtime by the interpreter. You don't have to compile your program before executing it. This is similar to PHP and PERL.
- **Interactive:** You can actually sit at a Python prompt and interact with the interpreter directly to write your scripts.

- **Object-Oriented:** Python supports Object-Oriented design or technique of programming that encapsulates code within objects, and creating and using classes and objects are downright easy.
- **A Beginner's Language:** Python is a beginner-friendly programming language and supports the development of a wide range of applications from simple text processing scripts to WWW browsers to games.

History of Python

Python was conceived in the late 1980s and was developed by Guido van Rossum—whose favorite comedy group at the time was Monty Python's Flying Circus—at the National Research Institute for Mathematics and Computer Science in the Netherlands. It has originated from other scripting languages such as ABC, Algol-68, C, C++, Modula-3, SmallTalk, Unix shell, and etc.

As Guido van Rossum started implementing Python, he was also reading the published scripts from a BBC comedy series from the 1970s, "Monty Python's Flying Circus". He thought he needed a name that was short, unique, and slightly mysterious; hence, the name Python.

Python is copyrighted. Like PERL, its source code is now available under the GNU General Public License (GPL). It is being maintained at the institute by a core development group, although Guido van Rossum still plays a vital role in ushering its progress.

Python Features

Python's features include the following:

Easy-to-learn: Python should be your first programming language because it will quickly teach you how to think like a programmer. It has few keywords, simple structure, and a clearly defined syntax. Indeed, it provides a stepping stone into the world of programming. That's why even students can pick up the language quickly.

Easy-to-read: Easy-to-read: Python put an emphasis on readability. Python doesn't adapt the usual symbols found in other programming languages such as dollar signs ($), semicolons (;), tides (~), and many other symbols used for accessing variables, code block definition, and pattern matching. So instead of memorizing the cryptic syntax that other languages present you, you will be able to focus on learning programming concepts and paradigms in Python. Moreover, it also serves as a backbone of Google; this scripting language uses lesser lines of code unlike C++ and Java. Python basics has been a big help in creating a solid base for the student's programming career ahead of C and C++.

Easy-to-maintain: Maintaining source code will always be a part of the software development lifecycle. Obviously, because Python is easy-to-learn and easy-to-read, it is not hard to conclude that it is also easy-to-maintain. In addition to its motivating advantages, when reviewing a script you wrote six months ago, you are less likely to get lost or require pulling out a reference book to get reacquainted with your software.

Extensive Libraries: Python has a huge impressive standard library. Its philosophy is batteries-included, and a standard Python distribution comes with built-in database functionality, a range of data persistence features, routines for interfacing with the operating system, website interfacing, email and networking tools, cryptography, data compression support, XML support, multithreading, regular expressions, unit testing, and the list goes on. In short, if you want to take a break from writing a bunch of matrix manipulation code and automate an operating system task, you don't have to switch language! Python's library is very portable and moreover, it is cross-platform compatible on UNIX, Windows, and Macintosh.

Interactive Mode: Python has support for an interactive mode which allows you to do interactive testing and debugging of code snippets. This is a good way to play around and try variations on syntax.

Databases: Python can provide interfaces to the majority of commercial databases.

GUI Programming: Python provides graphic user interface applications which can be created then ported to a wide variety of libraries, system calls, and window systems including Windows MFC, Macintosh, and the X

Window system of Unix. This is possible using Python's de-facto standard GUI library, Tkinter.

Portable: Python can run on a wide range of hardware platforms and a number of operating systems. It also has the same interface on all platforms.

Extendable: It is quite easy to add new built-in modules to Python. You can add low-level modules to its interpreter. These modules allow developers to add to or customize their tools to be more efficient.

Scalable: Python supports a better structure and support for large programs than shell scripting.

Apart from the aforementioned features, Python still has a lot of good features to offer, few are listed below:

- It can be used as a scripting language or can be compiled to byte-code when building large applications.
- It supports functional and structured programming methods as well as OOP.
- It offers very high-level dynamic data types and supports dynamic type checking.

11

- It can be integrated with ActiveX, C, C++, CORBA, COM, and Java, downright easy.
- It has an automatic garbage collection.

II. Variables and Data Types

Variables are used to store information to be referenced and manipulated by programs. These are nothing but reserved memory locations to store values. Therefore, when you create a variable, you reserve some space in memory. The interpreter allocates memory and decides what can be stored in the reserved memory based on the data type of a variable. Hence, you can store characters, integers, or decimals in these variables by assigning different data types to variables.

Variables in Python are considered as **objects**. Declaration of variables is not necessary before using them, or declares their type. Most variables in Python are local in scope to their own class or function. However, global variables can be declared with the global keyword.

The Rules

1. Variables names should start with a letter or an underscore.
   a. _underscore
   b. underscore_

2. The rest of your variable name may consist of letters, numbers, and underscores.

    a. password1

    b. n00b

    c. un_der_scores

3. Variable names are case sensitive.

    a. case_sensitive, CASE_SENSITIVE, and Case_Sensitive are different variables.

The Conventions

1. Readability is a MUST. Which of the following is easiest to read? I'm hoping you'll say the first example.

    a. python_puppet

    b. pythonpuppet

    c. pythonPuppet

2. Avoid using names that are too general or too wordy. Strike a good balance between the two.

    a. Bad: data_structure, my_list, info_map, dictionary_for_the_purpose_of_storing_data_representing_word_definitions

    b. Good: user_profile, menu_options, word_definitions

3. When using CamelCase names, capitalize all letters of an abbreviation (e.g. HTTPServer)
4. Avoid using the lowercase letter 'l', uppercase 'O', and uppercase 'I'. Why? To avoid confusion as the l and the I look a lot like each other and the number 1. And so is O and 0.

Assigning Values to Variables

Python variables need not to declare explicitly to reserve memory space. When you assign a value to a variable, the declaration happens automatically and instantly. The equal (=) sign is used to assign values to variables. The operand to the left of the assignment operator (=) is the name of the variable and the operand to the right of the assignment operator (=) is the value stored in the variable. For example:

```
#!usr/bin/python

name = 'Jane Doe'          # A string
age = 20                   #   An   integer
assignment
```

```
height = 170.18                    #    A    floating
point

print name
print age
print height
```

Here, "Jane Doe", 20, and 170.18 are the values assigned to name, age, and height variables respectively. The code written above produces the following result:

```
Jane Doe
20
170.18
```

Multiple Assignment

One of the cooler programming shortcuts in Python is it allows you to assign a single value to several variables simultaneously. This lets you initialize several variables at once, which you can reassign later in the program yourself, or through user input. For example:

```
#!usr/bin/python

a = b = c = 7

print a
print b
print c
```

Here, all three of the variables (a, b, and c) are assigned to the same memory location. They are each equal to the value of 7 as shown in the output below:

```
7
7
7
```

Moreover, Python also allows you to assign multiple objects to multiple variables within the same line. Each of these values can have different data type:

```
#!usr/bin/python

x, y, z = 'Jane Doe', 20, 170.18
```

```
print x
print y
print                                              z
```

Here, the variable x was assigned to the string "Jane Doe", the variable y was assigned to the integer 20, and the variable z was assigned to the float 170.18. Running the code yields the following output:

```
Jane Doe
20
170.18
```

The Multiple Assignment approach keep your lines of code down as it only takes up one line, but make sure you are not compromising readability for fewer lines of code.

Standard Data Types

In Python programming, every value stored in memory has a data type. For example, a person's age is stored as a numeric value, while his or her address is stored as alphanumeric characters. Python has different standard

18

data types that are used to determine the storage method for each of them and the operations possible on them. As everything is an object in Python, data types are actually classes and variables are instances (objects) of these classes.

Python has five standard data types:

- Numbers
- String
- List
- Tuple
- Dictionary

Numbers

Number data types store numeric values. Python numbers objects are created by the standard Python method. For example:

```
var1 = 7
var2 = 70
```

Type	Format	Description
int	a = 10	Signed Integer
long	a = 777L	(L) Long integers, can also be represented in octal and hexadecimal
float	a = 18.32	(.) Floating point real values
complex	a = 3.14J	(J) Contains integer in the range 0 to 255.

Oftentimes, using the standard Python number type is fine. Python will automatically convert a number from one type to another if needed. But under certain circumstances that a specific number type is needed (ie. complex, hexadecimal), format can be forced by using additional syntax in the table below:

Here are other examples of numbers:

int	long	float	complex
10	51924361L	0.0	3.14j
100	-0x19323L	15.20	45.j
-786	0122L	-21.9	9.322e-36j
-0x260	-052318172735L	-32.54e100	3e+26J
0x69	-4721885298529L	70.2-E12	4.53e-7j

Moreover, the type function returns information about how your data is stored within a variable. For example:

```
#!usr/bin/python

message = "Hello World"
number = 85
pi = 3.14159

print(type(message))     # Returns a string
print(type(number))      # Returns an integer
print(type(pi))          # Returns a float
```

Strings

Python strings are arrays of characters as they are formed by a list of characters represented in the quotation marks. Python lets you use either pairs of single or double quotes. In addition, subsets of strings can be taken using the slice operator ([ ] and [:]) with indexes starting at 0 in the beginning of the string and working their way from -1 at the end. The plus (+) sign is used as a string concatenation operator, while the asterisk (*) is used as a repetition operator. For example:

```
#!usr/bin/python

str = 'Python is fun!'
print str                   #    Prints    complete
string
print str[0]                #      Prints      first
character of the string
print str[4:10]             #   Prints   characters
starting from 5th to 10th
print str[5:]               #      Prints      string
starting from 6th character
print str * 2               #   Prints   string   two
times
print str + "TEST"          #   Prints   concatenated
string
```

Output:

```
Python is fun!
P
```

```
on is
n is fun!
Python is fun!Python is fun!
Python is fun!TEST
```

Moreover, Python allows you to format multiple strings and numbers using a special syntax. The curly braces ({ }) are placeholders that are substituted by the variables `element` and `count` in the final string. This compact syntax is meant to keep the code more compact and readable. For example:

```
print    "Item    {}    is    repeated    {}
times".format(element,count))
```

Python is currently transitioning to the format syntax above, but Python still allows to use the older syntax, which is being phased out, and is still seen in some example code:

```
print    "Item    %i    is    repeated    %i    times"%
(element,count)
```

Lists

Lists are the most frequent used and most versatile of Python's compound data types. Declaring a list is pretty straight forward. Items are separated by commas and enclosed within square brackets ([ ]). To some extent, lists are similar to arrays in C. One difference between them is that all the elements in a list do not need to be of the same type.

Lists work similarly to strings, the elements in a list can be accessed using the slice operator ([ ] and [:]) with indexes starting at 0 in the beginning of the list and working their way to end -1. The plus (+) sign is the list concatenation operator, and the asterisk (*) is the repetition operator. For example:

```
#!/usr/bin/python

list = [ 'abcde', 789, 3.14, 'jane', 70.2 ]
tiny_list = [ 456, 'jane' ]
```

```
print list                  #   Displays   complete
list
print list[0]               #    Displays    first
element of the list
print list[1:3]             #   Displays   elements
starting from 2nd till 3rd
print list[2:]              #   Displays   elements
starting from 3rd element
print tiny_list * 2         #  Displays  list  two
times
print list + tiny_list #              Displays
concatenated lists
```

Output:

```
['abcde', 789, 3.14, 'jane', 70.2]
abcde
[789, 3.14]
[3.14, 'jane', 70.2]
[456, 'jane', 456, 'jane']
['abcde',  789,  3.14,  'jane',  70.2,  456,
'jane']
```

25

Like other programming languages, Python allows you to assign a value to a specific element of the list using an index into the list. For example:

```
#!/usr/bin/python

list = [0, 1, 2, 3]

list[0] = 'Asparagus'
list[1] = 'Broccoli'
list[2] = 'Carrot'
list[3] = 'Dill'

print list[1]                    #         Outputs
Broccoli
```

Tuples

A tuple is another sequence data type that is similar to the list and can be manipulated in similar ways. A tuple consists of a number of values separated by commas.

26

However, unlike lists, tuples are enclosed within parentheses (( )).

Lists are represented in brackets ([ ]) and their elements and size can be changed. On the other hand, tuples are enclosed in parentheses (( )) and is fixed and cannot be updated. Therefore, tuples can be thought of as read-only lists. For example:

```
#!/usr/bin/python

tuple = ( 'abcde', 789, 3.14, 'jane', 70.2 )
tiny_tuple = ( 456, 'jane' )

print tuple                    #        Displays
complete tuple
print tuple[0]                 # Displays first
element of the list
print tuple[1:3]               #        Displays
elements starting from 2nd till 3rd
print tuple[2:]                #        Displays
elements starting from 3rd element
print tiny_tuple * 2           # Displays tuple
two times
print tuple + tiny_tuple       #        Displays
concatenated tuples
```

Output:

27

```
('abcde', 789, 3.14, 'jane', 70.2)
abcde
(789, 3.14)
(3.14, 'jane', 70.2)
(456, 'jane', 456, 'jane')
('abcde',   789,   3.14,   'jane',   70.2,   456,
'jane')
```

The following code is not allowed when using tuple, as we attempted to update it, which is invalid. Similar case is possible with lists:

```
#!/usr/bin/python

tuple = ( 'abcde', 789 , 3.14, 'jane', 70.2 )
list = [ 'abcde', 789 , 3.14, 'jane', 70.2 ]

tuple[2] = 1000              # Invalid syntax
with tuple
list[2] = 1000              #  Valid  syntax
with list
```

Dictionary

Python's dictionaries are kind of hash table type. They work like associative arrays or hashes found in Perl. Dictionaries are unordered and consist of key-value pairs. Each key is unique and can be almost any Python type, while the values can be any arbitrary Python object, but usually they are string, int, or float, or a list of these things. Like lists, dictionaries can easily be updated, can be shrunk, and grown as desired at run-time. Dictionaries are enclosed in curly braces ({ }), and values can be assigned and accessed using square braces ([ ]). For example:

```
#!/usr/bin/python

dict = {}
dict[1] = "This is one"
dict['two'] = "This is two"
tiny_dict    =    {'name':    'jane','code':1234,
'dept': 'IT'}

print dict[1]                    #  Prints  value
for 1 key
```

```
print dict['two']              #   Prints   value
for 'two' key
print tiny_dict                #             Prints
complete dictionary
print tiny_dict.keys()         # Prints  all  the
keys
print tiny_dict.values()       # Prints  all  the
values
```

Output:

```
This is one
This is two
{'dept': 'IT', 'code': 1234, 'name': 'jane'}
['dept', 'code', 'name']
['IT', 1234, 'jane']
```

Data Type Conversion

Python can do variable conversion automatically. But you can also use Python's built-in conversion functions to convert the data from one type to another.

Function	Description

int(x [,base])	Converts x to an integer. base specifies the base if x is a string.
long(x [,base])	Converts x to a long integer. base specifies the base if x is a string.
complex(real [,imag])	Creates a complex number.
str(x)	Converts object x to a string representation.
repr(x)	Converts object x to an expression string.
eval(str)	Evaluates a string and returns an object.
tuple(s)	Converts s to a tuple.
list(s)	Converts s to a list.
set(s)	Converts s to a set.
dict(d)	Creates a dictionary. d must be a sequence of (key,value) tuples.
frozenset(s)	Converts s to a frozen set.
chr(x)	Converts an integer to a character.
unichr(x)	Converts an integer to a Unicode character.
ord(x)	Converts a single character to its integer value.

hex(x)	Converts an integer to a hexadecimal string.
oct(x)	Converts an integer to an octal string.

III. Basic Operators

Operators are special symbols used in Python that can manipulate the value of operands. Consider the expression 3 + 4 = 7. Here, 3 and 4 are called operands and + is called operator.

Types of Operators

Python language has a number of operators which are classified below:

- Arithmetic Operators
- Comparison (Relational) Operators
- Assignment Operators
- Logical Operators
- Bitwise Operators
- Membership Operators
- Identity Operators

Let us have a look on all operators one by one.

Arithmetic Operators

Arithmetic operators take either literals or variables numerical values as operands then produce a single numerical value. The standard arithmetic operations used are addition (+), subtraction (-), multiplication (*), and division (/).

Assume variable **x** holds 50 and variable **y** holds 5, so:

Operator	Description	Description
+ Addition	Adds values on either side of the operator.	x + y = 55
- Subtraction	Subtracts right operand from left operand.	x - y = 45
* Multiplication	Multiplies values on either side of the operator.	x * y = 250
/ Division	Divides left operand by right operand.	x / y = 10
% Modulus	Divides left operand by right operand and returns remainder.	x % y = 0

** Exponent	Performs exponential (power) calculation on operators.	$x**y = 50$ to the power 5
// Floor Division	Also known as "integer division", which divides two numbers and removes the decimal point.	$9//2 = 4$ and $9.0//2.0 = 4$

Sample Program:

```
#!/usr/bin/python

x = 30
y = 6
z = 0

z = x + y
print "Line 1 - Value of z is ", z

z = x - y
print "Line 2 - Value of z is ", z

z = x * y
print "Line 3 - Value of z is ", z
```

```
z = x / y
print "Line 4 - Value of z is ", z


z = x % y
print "Line 5 - Value of z is ", z


x = 2
y = 4
z = x**y
print "Line 6 - Value of z is ", z
x = 50
y = 5
z = x//y
print "Line 7 - Value of z is ", z
```

Output:

```
Line 1 - Value of z is   36
Line 2 - Value of z is   24
Line 3 - Value of z is   180
Line 4 - Value of z is   5
Line 5 - Value of z is   0
Line 6 - Value of z is   16
Line 7 - Value of z is   10
```

Comparison Operators

Comparison operators, as their name implies, allow you to compare the values on either sides of them and decide the relation among them. They are also called Relational operators.

Assume variable x holds 50 and variable y holds 5, so:

Operator	Description	Example
==	If the values of two operands are equal, then the condition becomes true.	(x == y) is not true
!=	If values of two operands are not equal, then condition becomes true.	(x != y) is true
<>	If values of two operands are not equal, then condition becomes true.	(x <> y) is true. This is similar to != operator
>	If the value of left operand is greater than the value of	(x > y) is not true

	right operand, then condition becomes true.	
<	If the value of left operand is less than the value of right operand, then condition becomes true.	(x < y) is true
>=	If the value of left operand is greater than or equal to the value of right operand, then condition becomes true.	(x >= y) is not true
<=	If the value of left operand is less than or equal to the value of right operand, then condition becomes true.	(x <= y) is true

Sample Program:

```
#!/usr/bin/python

x = 30
y = 6

if ( x == y ):
     print "Line 1 - x is equal to y"
else:
     print "Line 1 - x is not equal to y"
```

```
if ( x != y ):
      print "Line 2 - x is not equal to y"
else:
      print "Line 2 - x is equal to y"


if ( x <> y ):
      print "Line 3 - x is not equal to y"
else:
      print "Line 3 - x is equal to y"


if ( x < y ):
      print "Line 4 - x is less than y"
else:
      print "Line 4 - x is not less than y"


if ( x > y ):
      print "Line 5 - x is greater than y"
else:
      print "Line 5 - x is not greater than y"


x = 2
y = 4
if ( x <= y ):
      print "Line 6 - x is either less than or
equal to y"
else:
      print "Line 6 - x is neither less than
nor equal to y"
```

```
if ( y >= x ):
      print "Line 7 - x is either greater than
or equal to y"
else:
      print "Line 7 - x is neither greater
than nor equal to y"
```

Output:

```
Line 1 - x is not equal to y
Line 2 - x is not equal to y
Line 3 - x is not equal to y
Line 4 - x is not less than y
Line 5 - x is greater than y
Line 6 - x is either less than or equal to y
Line 7 - x is either greater than or equal to
y
```

Logical Operators

A Boolean expression (or logical expression) typically used to evaluate whether two or more expressions are true or not. The following logical operators are supported by Python which yields either True or False:

Assume variable **x** holds 50 and variable **y** holds 5, so:

Operator	Description	Example
and Logical AND	True if both are true	(x and y) is true.
or Logical OR	True if at least one is true	(x or y) is true.
not Logical NOT	True only if false	Not (x and y) is false.

Assignment Operators

Equal (=) is the basic assignment operator. This assigns the value of its right operand to its left operand. Like this, **a** = **b** assigns the value of b to a. The other assignment operators are usually shorthand for standard operations, as shown in the following definitions and examples.

Assume variable **x** holds 50 and variable **y** holds 5, so:

Operator	Description	Example

41

=	Assigns a value to a variable (left operand).	z = x + y assigns value of x + y into z
+= Add AND	Adds the value of the right operand to a variable and assigns the result to the variable.	z += x is equivalent to z = z + x
-= Subtract AND	Subtracts the value of the right operand from a variable and assigns the result to the variable.	z -= x is equivalent to z = z - x
*= Multiply AND	Multiplies a variable by the value of the right operand and assigns the result to the variable.	z *= x is equivalent to z = z * x
/= Divide AND	Divides a variable by the value of the right operand and assigns the result to the variable.	z /= x is equivalent to z = z / x
%= Modulus AND	Divides a variable by the value of the right operand and assigns the remainder to the variable.	z %= x is equivalent to z = z % x
**= Exponent AND	Performs exponential (power) calculation on operators and assigns value to the variable.	z **= x is equivalent to z = z ** x
//=	Performs floor division on	z //= x is

Floor Division	operators and assigns value to the variable.	equivalent to z = z // x

Sample Program:

- -

```
#!/usr/bin/python


x = 30
y = 6
z = 0


z = x + y
print "Line 1 - Value of z is ", z


z += x
print "Line 2 - Value of z is ", z


z *= x
print "Line 3 - Value of z is ", z


z /= x
print "Line 4 - Value of z is ", z


z = 2
z %= x
print "Line 5 - Value of z is ", z


z **= x
```

```
print "Line 6 - Value of z is ", z

z //= x
print "Line 7 - Value of z is ", z
```

Output:

```
Line 1 - Value of z is   36
Line 2 - Value of z is   66
Line 3 - Value of z is   1980
Line 4 - Value of z is   66
Line 5 - Value of z is   2
Line 6 - Value of z is   1073741824
Line 7 - Value of z is   35791394
```

Bitwise Operators

The bitwise operators are widely used to create, manipulate, and read sequences of flags, which are like binary variables. Assume if `x = 60;` and `y = 13;` Now in binary format they will be as follows:

x   =   0011 1100

y   =   0000 1101

----

x&y	=	0000 1100
x|y	=	0011 1101
x^y	=	0011 0001
~x	=	1100 0011

The following Bitwise operators are supported by Python language:

Operator	Description	Example
& Binary AND	Each bit of the result is 1 if the corresponding bit of x AND of y is 1, otherwise it's 0.	(x & y) = 12 (means 0000 1100)
| Binary OR	Each bit of the result is 0 if the corresponding bit of x AND of y is 0, otherwise it's 1.	(x | y) = 61 (means 0011 1101)
^ Binary XOR	Each bit of the result is the same as the corresponding bit in x if that bit in y is 0, and it's the complement of the bit in x if that bit in y is 1.	(x ^ y) = 49 (means 0011 0001)
~ Binary Ones	Returns the complement of x,	(~a) = -61 (means 1100

Complement	which is the number you get by switching each 1 for a 0 and each 0 for a 1.	0011 in 2's complement form due to a signed binary number)
<< Binary Left Shift	Outputs x with the bits shifted to the left by y places (and new bits on the right-hand-side are zeros).	$x << 2 = 240$ (means 1111 0000)
>> Binary Right Shift	Outputs x with the bits shifted to the right by y places.	$x >> 2 = 15$ (means 0000 1111)

Sample Program:

```
#!/usr/bin/python

x = 60                  # 60 = 0011 1100
y = 13                  # 13 = 0000 1101
z = 0


z = x & y;              # 12 = 0000 1100
print "Line 1 - Value of z is ", z


z = x | y;              # 61 = 0011 1101
print "Line 2 - Value of z is ", z


z = x ^ y;              # 49 = 0011 0001
```

```
print "Line 3 - Value of z is ", z

z = ~x;                        # -61 = 1100 0011
print "Line 4 - Value of z is ", z

z = x << 2;                    #    240    =    1111
0000
print "Line 5 - Value of z is ", z

z = x >> 2;                    # 15 = 0000 1111
print "Line 6 - Value of z is ", z
```

- -

~

Output:

- -

```
Line 1 - Value of z is   12
Line 2 - Value of z is   61
Line 3 - Value of z is   49
Line 4 - Value of z is   -61
Line 5 - Value of z is   240
Line 6 - Value of z is   15
```

- -

~

Membership Operators

47

Membership operators, as the name implies, are used to validate the membership of a value. These are used to find out whether a value is a member of a sequence such as string or list. Membership operators are of two types:

Operator	Description	Example
in	Evaluates to true if a value exists in a sequence, otherwise false.	x in y This results in a 1 if x is a member of sequence y.
not	Evaluates to true if a value does not exist in a sequence, otherwise false.	x not in y This results in a 1 if x is not a member of sequence y.

Sample Program:

```
#!/usr/bin/python
x = 11
y = 8

list = [ 2, 4, 6, 8, 10 ];

if ( x in list ):
    print "Line 1 - x is available in the
given list"
```

48

```
else:
    print "Line 1 - x is not available in the
given list"

if ( y not in list ):
    print "Line 2 - y is not available in the
given list"
else:
    print "Line 2 - y is available in the
given list"

x = 2
if ( x in list ):
    print "Line 3 - x is available in the
given list"
else:
    print "Line 3 - x is not available in the
given list"
```

Output:

```
Line 1 - x is not available in the given list
Line 2 - y is available in the given list
Line 3 - x is available in the given list
```

Identity operators verify if two variables point to the same memory location or not. There are two Identity operators as explained below:

Operator	Description	Example
is	Results to true if the operands on either side of the operator point to same memory location, otherwise false.	x is y This results in 1 if id(x) equals id(y).
is not	Returns true if both the operand point to different memory location, otherwise false.	x is not y This results in 1 if id(x) is not equal to id(y).

Sample Program:

```
#!/usr/bin/python
x = 10
y = 10

if ( x is y ):
    print "Line 1 - x and y have same
identity"
else:
```

```
      print "Line 1 - x and y do not have same
identity"

if ( id(x) == id(y) ):
      print "Line 2 - x and y have same
identity"
else:
      print "Line 2 - x and y do not have same
identity"

y = 20
if ( x is y ):
      print "Line 3 - x and y have same
identity"
else:
      print "Line 3 - x and y do not have same
identity"

if ( x is not y ):
      print "Line 4 - x and y do not have same
identity"
else:
      print "Line 4 - x and y have same
identity"
```

When you execute the above program, it yields the following result:

```
Line 1 - x and y have same identity
Line 2 - x and y have same identity
Line 3 - x and y do not have same identity
Line 4 - x and y do not have same identity
```

Operators Precedence

The table below lists all operators from highest precedence to lowest.

Operator	Description
**	Exponentiation (raise to the power)
~, +, -	Complement, unary plus and minus (method names for the last two are +@ and -@)
*, /, %, //	Multiply, divide, modulo, and floor division
+ -	Addition and subtraction
>>, <<	Right and left bitwise shift
&	Bitwise 'AND'
^, |	Bitwise exclusive `OR' and regular

	`OR'
<=, < >, >=	Comparison operators
<>, ==, !=	Equality operators
=, %=, /=, //=, -=, +=, *=, **=	Assignment operators
is, is not	Identity operators
in, not in	Membership operators
not, or, and	Logical operators

Operator precedence affects how an expression is evaluated. For example, `x = 8 + 4 * 3;` here, x is assigned 20, not 36 because operator * has higher precedence than +, so it first multiplies 4*3 and then adds into 8.

Sample Program:

```
#!/usr/bin/python

a = 30
b = 20
c = 25
d = 15
e = 0
```

53

```
e = (a + b) * c / d                    # (  30  *
25 ) / 15
print "Value of (a + b) * c / d is ", e

e = ((a + b) * c) / d                  # (30 * 25
) / 15
print "Value of ((a + b) * c) / d is ", e

e = (a + b) * (c / d);                 #   (30)  *
(25/5)
print "Value of (a + b) * (c / d) is ", e

e = a + (b * c) / d;                   #    30   +
(250/5)
print "Value of a + (b * c) / d is ", e
```

Output:

```
Value of (a + b) * c / d is  83
Value of ((a + b) * c) / d is  83
Value of (a + b) * (c / d) is  50
Value of a + (b * c) / d is  63
```

IV. Control Flow Statements

A program's control flow is the sequence or order of program execution. In Python programming, the control flow is controlled by conditional statements, loops, and function calls. This section tackles the if statement, and for and while loops; functions and exceptions are covered later in the next chapters.

The if Statement

Like in other programming languages, Python's if statement executes a set of statements conditionally, based on the value of a logical expression. The Python compound statement if, which comprises of `if`, `elif`, and `else` clauses, allows you to execute blocks of codes conditionally.

Syntax:

- -

```
if expression:
    statement(s)
```

55

```
elif expression:
    statement(s)
elif expression:
    statement(s)
...
else:
    statement(s)
```

The `elif` and `else` clauses are optional. Compared to other programming languages, Python does not support a `switch` statement; therefore, you must use if, elif, and else for all conditional processing.

Sample Program:

```
#!/usr/bin/python

var = 150
if var == 200:
      print "1 - Got a true expression value"
      print var
elif var == 150:
      print "2 - Got a true expression value"
      print var
elif var == 100:
      print "3 - Got a true expression value"
```

```
        print var
else:
        print "4 - Got a false expression value"
        print var

print "Good bye!"
```

Output:

```
2 - Got a true expression value
150
Good bye!
```

The while Statement

In Python programming language, a `while` loop runs a given condition is true and execute the program block.

Syntax:

```
while expression:
        statement(s)
```

While other programming languages that use curly braces ({ }) or parentheses (( )) to group statements, Python uses indentation as its method of grouping statements. All the statements indented by the same number of character spaces after a programming construct are considered to be part of a single block of code.

Sample Program:

```
#!/usr/bin/python

count = 0

while ( count < 9 ):
      print 'The count is:', count
      count = count + 1

print "Good bye!"
```

Output:

```
The count is: 0
The count is: 1
The count is: 2
```

```
The count is: 3
The count is: 4
The count is: 5
The count is: 6
The count is: 7
The count is: 8
Good bye!
```

The block here, composing of the print and increment statements, is iterated until count is no longer less than 9. With each loop, the current value of the index count is displayed and then incremented by 1.

✏️ Take Note

The while loop is the iteration that might not ever run. When the condition is tested and evaluates to false, the program will skip the loop body and will execute the first statement after the while loop.

The for Loop

The `for..in` statement is another looping statement that has the ability to iterate over the items of any sequence, such as a list or a string.

Syntax:

```
for it_var in sequence:
      statements(s)
```

✎ Take Note

The `in` *keyword is part of the for loop syntax and is functionally unrelated to the in operator used for membership testing. A for loop can also have an* `else` *clause,* `break`, *and* `continue` *statements.*

Sample Program:

```
#!/usr/bin/python

for letter in 'Python': # First Example
      print 'Current Letter :', letter

fruits = [ 'apple', 'banana', 'cherry' ]

for fruit in fruits: # Second Example
      print 'Current fruit :', fruit

print "Good bye!"
```

Output:

```
Current          Letter          :              P
Current          Letter          :              y
Current          Letter          :              t
Current          Letter          :              h
Current          Letter          :              o
Current          Letter          :              n
Current          fruit        :           apple
Current          fruit        :           banana
Current          fruit        :           cherry
Good bye!
```

Here are the other examples of how to use the for loop statement:

Example #1: Iteration using `range()` function:

```
#!/usr/bin/python


#range(5) returns [0, 1, 2, 3, 4]


for my_var in range(5):
     print 'Iteration number : ' + str(my_var
+ 1)
```

Output:

61

```
Iteration number : 1
Iteration number : 2
Iteration number : 3
Iteration number : 4
Iteration number : 5
```

Example #2: Iterating through a String:

```
#!/usr/bin/python

my_str = 'Python Rocks'

for my_var in my_str:
      print 'Letter: ' + my_var.upper()
```

Output:

```
Letter:                                      P
Letter:                                      Y
Letter:                                      T
Letter:                                      H
Letter:                                      O
Letter:                                      N
Letter:
```

```
Letter:                                    R
Letter:                                    O
Letter:                                    C
Letter:                                    K
Letter: S
```

- -

Example #3: Iterating through a List:

```python
#!/usr/bin/python

my_list = [ 2, 4, 6, 8 ]

for my_var in my_list:
    print 'Cube of ' + str ( my_var ) + ' =
' + str ( my_var ** 3 )
```

Output:

```
Cube of 2 = 8

Cube of 4 = 64

Cube of 6 = 216

Cube of 8 = 512
```

Example #4: Iterating through a Tuple:

```python
#!/usr/bin/python

my_tuple = ( 'Ice Cream', 'Cake', 'Pizza',
'Hamburger' )

for my_var in my_tuple:
      print 'I want to eat ' + my_var + '!'
```

Output:

```
I want to eat Ice Cream!
I want to eat Cake!
I want to eat Pizza!
I want to eat Hamburger!
```

Example #5: Iterating through Key-Values in a Dictionary

```python
#!/usr/bin/python

dict = { 'Italy': 'Juventus', 'Germany':
'Bayern Munich', 'England': 'Leicester City',
'Spain': 'Barcelona' }
```

64

```
for (country, club) in dict.items():
    print club + ' -> ' + country
```

Output:

```
Bayern Munich -> Germany

Juventus -> Italy

Leicester City -> England

Barcelona -> Spain
```

The break and continue Statement

Oftentimes, the `break` statement is used inside an if statement in order to prematurely exit from the for loop based on certain condition. Whereas, `continue` statement will jump to the next iteration without executing subsequent block of code, based on a condition.

Syntax:

```
for variable_name in python_iterable_object :
    statement(s)
```

```
if (condition) :
        statement(s)
        break


if (condition) :
        statement(s)
        continue
```

Example #1: break statement to stop counting at 5

```
#!/usr/bin/python

for my_var in range(1, 11):
    if my_var > 7 :
        break

    print 'Number ' + str(my_var)
```

Output:

```
Number                                    1
Number                                    2
Number                                    3
Number                                    4
Number                                    5
```

Here, my_var is always kept in check whether it is greater than 7. Until it is less or equal to 7, if condition evaluates to false and print statement is executed. Once it reaches 8, condition evaluates to true which then executes break statement, hence exiting from the loop. In the end, we have all the numbers less or equal to 7.

Example #2: continue statement to print only even numbers

```
#!/usr/bin/python

for my_var in range(1, 11):
    if my_var % 2 != 0 :
        continue

    print 'Number ' + str(my_var) + ' is an
even number'
```

Output:

```
Number 2 is an even number
```

```
Number 4 is an even number

Number 6 is an even number

Number 8 is an even number

Number 10 is an even number
```

In above example, the expression `my_var % 2 == 0` checks if `my_var` is an even or odd number. Whenever the condition returns false, print statement is executed. When it returns true, continue statement is executed. The program jumps to next iteration skipping the execution of further statements; hence, print statement does not execute. As a result, all the even numbers are printed on the terminal.

The for...else Loop

Well, this might seem to be very unusual, but we do have an optional `else` block in for loop statement in Python. This else block gets executed only when break statement is not executed. If there is no break statement in the code, else block will always execute.

Sample Program:

```
#!/usr/bin/python

my_num = 7

for myVar in range(12):
    if myVar == my_num:
        print 'Found!'
        break

    else:
        continue

else:
    print 'Not found!'
```

Output:

```
Found!
```

Here, we loop through a list of 12 integers and compare if the number is `my_num`. If the number matches, we print Found! and execute break statement.

V. Functions

Function is a block of related statements that perform a specific task. Functions help break our program into smaller and modular chunks. As our program grows larger and larger, functions make it more organized and manageable. Moreover, it avoids repetition and makes code reusable.

Like other programming languages, Python gives you many built-in functions such as `print()`, but you can also create your own functions. These functions are called user-defined functions.

Defining a Function

The following are simple rules on defining a function in Python:

- Functions start with the keyword **def** followed by the function name and parentheses (( )).

- Any input (arguments or parameters) must be placed inside the parentheses. You can also define parameters inside these parentheses.
- The first statement of a function, the docstring or documentation string which describes what the function does, can be an optional statement.
- The code block inside every function starts with a colon (:) and is indented.
- An optional return statement to return a value from the function back to the caller.

Syntax:

```
def function_name( parameters ) :
    "function_docstring"
    function suite
    return [expression]
```

Sample Program:

```
#!/usr/bin/python

def getMessage():
    # block belonging to the function
```

```
    print 'Hello World'
    # End of function

getMessage()                        # call the
function
getMessage()                        # call the
function again
```

Output:

```
Hello World
Hello World
```

We define a function called `getMessage` using the syntax as explained before. This function has no parameters and therefore there are no variables declared within the parentheses. Parameters to functions are just input to the function so that we can pass variables with different values to it and get back corresponding results.

When you define a function, you only give it a name, which specifies the parameters that are to be included in the function and structures the blocks of code. Once the basic structure of a function is completed, it will execute when you call it from another function or directly from the Python prompt. Notice that we call the same function twice which means we do not have to write the same code again.

Scope of Variables

The variable's accessibility depends on where you have declared it. The scope of a variable identifies the part of the program where you can access a certain identifier. There are two basic scopes of variables in Python:

- Global variables
- Local variables

Global vs. Local Variables

Variables that are declared inside a function definition have a local scope, while those declared outside have a global scope. This means that local variables can be accessed only inside the function in which they are declared, whereas global variables can be accessed anywhere in the program body by all functions. When you call a function, the variables defined inside it are brought into scope.

Sample Program:

```python
#!/usr/bin/python

total = 0;                      # This is global
variable.

# Function definition is here
def add_num( arg1, arg2 ):
      # Add both the parameters and return
them."
      total = arg1 + arg2;    # Here total is
local variable.
      print 'Inside the function local total :
', total
      return total;

# Now you can call sum function
add_num ( 20, 30 );
print 'Outside the function global total : ',
total
```

Output:

```
Inside the function local total : 50
Outside the function global total : 0
```

Passing by Reference Vs. Passing by Value

In Python language, all parameters (arguments) are passed by reference. It means if you change what a parameter refers to inside a function, the change also reflects back in the calling function.

Sample Program:

```python
#!/usr/bin/python


# Function definition is here
def changeMe ( my_list ):
    "This changes a passed list into this
function"
    my_list.append([ 2, 4 ,6 ,8 ]);
    print "Values inside the function:  ",
my_list
    return

# Now you can call changeMe function
my_list = [10, 20, 30];
changeMe( my_list );
```

```
print "Values outside the function: ", my_list
```

Here, we are maintaining reference of the passed object and inserting the values in the same object. Hence, this would yield the following result:

```
Values inside the function: [10, 20, 30, [2, 4
,6 ,8]]
Values outside the function: [10, 20, 30, [2,
4 ,6 ,8]]
```

Example below shows an argument that is being passed by reference and the reference is replaced inside the called function.

```
#!/usr/bin/python

# Function definition is here
def changeMe( my_list ):
      'This  changes  a  passed  list  into  this
function'
      my_list = [ 2, 4, 6, 8 ]; # This would
assign new reference in my_list
      print  'Values  inside  the  function:  ',
my_list
```

```
    return
```

```
# Now you can call changeMe function
my_list = [ 10, 20, 30];
changeMe( my_list );
print 'Values outside the function: ', my_list
```

The parameter `my_list` is local to the function `changeMe`. Altering `my_list` inside the function does not affect `my_list`. It then displays the following output:

```
Values inside the function: [2, 4, 6, 8]
Values outside the function: [10, 20, 30]
```

Function Arguments

You can call a function by using the following types of formal arguments:

- Default arguments
- Keyword arguments
- Required arguments
- Variable-length arguments

Default Arguments

Function arguments can have default values in Python. By using the assignment operator (=), we can provide a default value to an argument.

Sample Program:

```python
#!/usr/bin/python

def greet( name, msg = "Good morning!" ):
    """
    This function greets to
    the person with the
    provided message.

    If message is not provided,
    it defaults to "Good
    morning!"
    """

    print "Hello", name + ', ' + msg

greet("Patty")
greet("Marlon", "How do you do?")
```

Output:

```
Hello Patty, Good morning!
Hello Marlon, How do you do?
```

Keyword Arguments

When a function is called with some values, these values get assigned to the arguments according to their position.

For example, in the above function `greet()`, when we called it as `greet("Marlon","How do you do?")`, the value "Marlon" gets assigned to the argument name and same with "How do you do?" to msg.

Python allows functions to be called through keyword arguments. When a function is called in this manner, the order (position) of the arguments can be altered. Following calls to the above function are all valid and yield the same output.

Sample Code:

```
#!/usr/bin/python

def greet( name, msg ):
     print "Hello", name + ', ' + msg

greet( msg = "Good morning!", name = "Patty" )
```

Output:

```
Hello Patty, Good morning!
```

Required Arguments

Required arguments need to have a correct positional order. Here, the number of arguments given in the function call should exactly match with the function definition.

To call the function `greet()`, you definitely need to pass one argument, otherwise it gives a syntax error as follows:

```
#!/usr/bin/python
```

```
def greet( name ):
     print "Hello", name


greet()
```

Output:

```
Traceback (most recent call last):
  File "main.py", line 6, in <module>
    greet()
TypeError: greet() takes exactly 1 argument (0
given)
```

Arbitrary Arguments

Sometimes, the number of arguments that will be passed into a function is unknown. Hence, Python lets us handle this kind of situation through function calls with arbitrary number of arguments. To denote this kind of argument, use an asterisk (*) before the parameter name. For example:

Sample Code:

```python
#!/usr/bin/python

def greet( *names ):
    """This function greets all
    the person in the names tuple."""

    # names is a tuple with arguments
    for name in names:
        print("Hello", name)

greet("Spring", "Summer", "Fall", "Winter")
```

Output:

```
Hello Spring
Hello Summer
Hello Fall
Hello Winter
```

In the given example, the function is called with multiple arguments. These arguments get wrapped into a tuple before passing them into the function. Inside the function, a for loop is used to retrieve all the arguments back.

VI. Exceptions

When writing a program, more often than not, we will encounter errors. Error resulted from not following the proper structure or syntax of the language is called syntax error or parsing error. For example:

```
File        "main.py",        line        1
   if           a              <          3
        ^
SyntaxError: invalid syntax
```

Here, a missing column from the statement caused a syntax error.

Errors can also happen during runtime and these ones are called exceptions. They happen, for example, when a file we try to open is not found (`FileNotFoundError`), dividing a number by zero (`ZeroDivisionError`), module we try to import does not exist (`ImportError`), etc.

Python has many built-in exceptions which allow your program to yield an error when something in it goes wrong. When these exceptions happen, it causes the current process to forcefully stop and passes it to the calling process until it is handled. If not handled, our program will crash.

Sub-Title

Like in major programming languages, exceptions can be handled using a `try` block in Python. A critical operation which can raise exception is placed inside the try statement and the code that handles exception is written in except clause. It is now up to you, what actions you perform once you have caught the exception. For example:

- -

```
#!/usr/bin/python

import sys                # import module sys to
get the type of exception

random_list = ['a', 0, 2]

for entry in random_list:
```

```
try:
    print "The entry is", entry
    r = 1/int(entry)
    break
except:
    print
"Oops!",sys.exc_info()[0],"occurred."
    print "Next entry."

print "The reciprocal of", entry, "is", r
```

Output:

```
The          entry          is          a
Oops!    <type    'exceptions.ValueError'>
occurred.
Next                              entry.
The          entry          is          0
Oops! <type  'exceptions.ZeroDivisionError'>
occurred.
Next                              entry.
The          entry          is          2
The reciprocal of 2 is 0
```

Here, we loop until the user inputs an integer that has an acceptable reciprocal. The part that can cause exception is placed inside try clause. If no exception occurs, except

85

block is skipped and normal flow continues. Otherwise, it is caught by the except block.

In this program, we print the exception name using ex_info() function, which can be found inside sys module, and ask the user to try again. We can see that the values 'a' and '1.3' produces the ValueError error and '0' ZeroDivisionError.

Catching Specific Exceptions

In the previous example, we did not mention any exception in the except clause. This is a bad practive because it will catch all exceptions, thus handling every case in the same way. We can specify which exceptions an except clause will catch. A tuple of values can be used to specify multiple exceptions in an except clause.

Syntax:

```
try:
    # do something
    pass
```

```python
except ValueError:
    # handle ValueError exception
    pass

except ( TypeError, ZeroDivisionError ):
    # handle multiple exceptions
    # TypeError and ZeroDivisionError
    pass

except:
    # handle all other exceptions
    pass
```

---

try...finally

In Python, the try block can have an optional finally clause, which is executed no matter what, and is commonly used to release external resources. For example, we may be connected to a remote data center via the network or working with a file or working with a Graphical User Interface (GUI).

In all these circumstances, we should clean up the resource once used, whether it was successful or not. These actions (closing a file, GUI or disconnecting from network) are performed in the finally clause to guarantee execution.

Sample Code:

```
try:
# perform file operations
    f = open( "test.txt", encoding = 'utf-8' )

finally:
    f.close()
```

This kind of construct ensures that the file is closed even if an exception occurs.

VII. Classes and Objects

Since the birth of Python, it has always been an object-oriented language. Therefore, creating and using classes and objects are made easier. This chapter aims for you to become an expert in using Python's object-oriented programming (OOP) support.

However, if you do not have any previous experience with OOP, you may want to consult an introductory course first or at least a tutorial of some sort in order for you to have a basic knowledge on the subject matter.

Here is small introduction of Object-Oriented Programming (OOP) to bring you at speed:

Overview of OOP Terminology

- **Class:** An extensible program-code-template definition of the methods and variables in a particular kind of object. It is accessed using dot (.) notation.

- **Instance:** An individual object of a particular class. For example, an object obj that belongs to a class Square is an instance of the class Square.
- **Instantiation:** The creation of an instance.
- **Inheritance:** When an object or class is based on another object or class, using the same implementation.
- **Method:** A procedure associated with a class.
- **Object:** A unique instance of a class where the object can be comprised of variables, functions, and data structures.
- **Class variable:** A variable that is shared with all instances of a class. Each object of the class does not have its own copy of a class variable. Rather, each object shares the one and only copy of that class variable – and any changes made to that copy are reflected by all of the objects of that class.
- **Instance variable:** A variable which belongs only to the current instance of a class. Every object has its own copy of the instance variables.
- **Data member:** May be of any type, including classes already defined, pointers to objects of any type, or even references to objects of any type.

- **Operator overloading:** It allows same operator to have different meaning according to the context.

Creating Classes

The class keyword creates a new class definition.

Syntax:

```
class ClassName:
    'Optional class documentation string'
    class_suite
```

- Like the function, class, too, has a documentation string, which is accessible using ClassName.__doc__.
- The class_suite comprises of all the component statements which define class members, data attributes, and functions.

Sample Python Class:

```
class Employee:
```

```python
    'Common base class for all employees'
    emp_count = 0

    def __init__ ( self, name, salary ) :
        self.name = name
        self.salary = salary
        Employee.emp_count += 1

    def displayCount ( self ) :
        print   "Total   Employee   %d"   %
Employee.emp_count

    def displayEmployee ( self ) :
        print  "Name  :  ",  self.name,  ",
Salary: ", self.salary
```

- The variable emp_count is a class variable whose value is shared among all instances of a this class. You can access this as Employee.emp_count from within the class or outside the class.

- The first method __init__() is a special method. It is also called class constructor or initialization method that Python calls upon the creation of a new instance of a class.

- Declaring other class methods is like normal functions with the exception that the first argument to each method is self. Python adds the self argument to the list for you; you do not have to include it when you call the methods.

Creating Instance Objects

To create instances of a class, call the class using its class name and pass in any arguments its __init__ method accepts.

Syntax:

```
"This would create first object of Employee
class"
employee1 = Employee ( "Patty", 5000 )


"This would create second object of Employee
class"
employee2 = Employee ( "Marlon", 7000 )
```

Accessing Attributes

The object's attributes can be accessed through the dot (.) notation with object. For example:

```
employee1.displayEmployee()
employee2.displayEmployee()
print "Total Employee %d" % Employee.emp_count
```

Now, putting all the concepts together:

```
#!/usr/bin/python

class Employee:
    'Common base class for all employees'
    emp_count = 0

    def __init__(self, name, salary):
        self.name = name
        self.salary = salary
        Employee.emp_count += 1

    def displayCount(self):
        print "Total    Employee    %d"    %
Employee.emp_count

    def displayEmployee(self):
```

```
      print "Name : ", self.name,   ", Salary:
", self.salary


"This would create first object of Employee
class"
employee1 = Employee("Patty", 5000)


"This would create second object of Employee
class"
employee2 = Employee("Marlon", 7000)


employee1.displayEmployee()
employee2.displayEmployee()
print      "Total      Employee:      %d"      %
Employee.emp_count
```

Output:

```
Name     :      Patty    ,   Salary:      5000
Name     :      Marlon   ,   Salary:      7000
Total Employee: 2
```

Python allows you to add, delete, or edit attributes of classes and objects at any time:

```
employee1.age = 27          #  Add  an
'age' attribute
employee1.age = 28          #  Modify
'age' attribute
del employee1.age           #  Delete
'age' attribute
```

You can use the following functions to access the attributes in lieu of using the normal statements to access attributes:

- The getattr (object, name[, default]) − to access the attribute of an object.
- The hasattr (object, name) − to check if an attribute exists or not.
- The setattr (object, name, value) − to set an attribute. If attribute does not exist, then it would be created.
- The delattr (object, name) − to delete an attribute.

Sample Code:

```
hasattr ( employee1, 'age' )          #    Returns
true if 'age' attribute exists
getattr ( employee1, 'age' )          #    Returns
value of 'age' attribute
setattr ( employee1, 'age', 27 )      #       Set
attribute 'age' at 8
delattr ( empl, 'age' )               #    Delete
attribute 'age'
```

Class Inheritance

One of the major benefits of OOP is reuse of code and one of the ways this is achieved is through the inheritance. You can create a class (child class) by deriving it from a preexisting class by listing the parent class in parentheses after the new class name. The child class, therefore, inherits the attributes of its parent class, then the child class can use and access these attributes as if they were declared in the child class. Furthermore, a child class can also override data members and methods from the parent.

Syntax:

```python
class ChildClass (ParentClass1[, ParentClass2,
...]):
    'Optional class documentation string'
    class_suite
```

Sample Program:

```python
#!/usr/bin/python

class ParentClass :                          #
define parent class
    parentAttr = 100
    def __init__ ( self ):
        print "Calling parent constructor"

    def parentMethod ( self ) :
        print 'Calling parent method'

    def setAttr ( self, attr ) :
        ParentClass.parentAttr = attr

    def getAttr ( self ):
        print      "Parent     attribute     :",
ParentClass.parentAttr

class ChildClass ( ParentClass ):            #
define child class
```

```
    def __init__ ( self ):
        print "Calling child constructor"

    def childMethod ( self ) :
        print 'Calling child method'

cc = ChildClass()                               #
instance of child
cc.childMethod()                                #
child calls its method
cc.parentMethod()                               #
calls parent's method
cc.setAttr(500)                                 #
again call parent's method
cc.getAttr()                                    #
again call parent's method
```

Output:

```
Calling          child          constructor
Calling          child          method
Calling          parent         method
Parent attribute : 500
```

Overriding Methods

99

Python allows you to override your parent class methods. The main reason for overriding parent's methods is because you may want a different or special functionality in your subclass.

Sample Program:

```
#!/usr/bin/python

class ParentClass:                          #
define parent class
   def myMethod ( self ) :
      print 'Calling parent method'

class ChildClass ( ParentClass ) :          #
define child class
   def myMethod ( self ) :
      print 'Calling child method'

cc = ChildClass()                           #
instance of child
cc.myMethod()                               #
child calls overridden method
```

Output:

```
Calling child method
```

VI. What's Next?

If you have read this book thoroughly until now and practiced writing a number of programs, then you are already comfortable and familiar with Python. You have probably created some Python programs to try out stuff and to exercise your Python skills as well. If you have not done it yet, you should start now. The question now is 'What's next?'.

I would suggest that you tackle this problem:

> Create your own command-line address-book program which you can add, edit, delete, or search for your contacts such as family, friends, and colleagues, and their information such as email address and/or phone number. Details must be stored for later retrieval.

Once you are able to do this, congratulations, you can claim to be a Python programmer! Thank you for picking up and reading this book. Till our next tutorial, happy coding!

About the Author

Patty Belle is a programmer at daytime and a writer at night. Her passion for reading and encouraging people to reach their full potential inspired her on writing books. When she isn't in front of the computer, she daydreams, eats, travels, photographs, and lives life to the fullest.